The Story of

ROMAN INVADERS

Jane Shuter

Raintree

www.raintreepublishers.co.uk
Visit our website to find out more information about **Raintree** books.

To order:
 ☎ Phone 44 (0) 1865 888112
📄 Send a fax to 44 (0) 1865 314091
💻 Visit the Raintree Bookshop at **www.raintreepublishers.co.uk** to browse our catalogue and order online.

First published in Great Britain by Raintree, Halley Court, Jordan Hill, Oxford OX2 8EJ, part of Pearson Education. Raintree is a registered trademark of Pearson Education Ltd.

Editorial: Sian Smith
Design: Kimberley R. Miracle, Big Top and Joanna Hinton-Malivoire
Picture research: Ruth Blair
Production: Duncan Gilbert
Illustrated by Beehive Illustration
Originated by Dot Gradations

Printed and bound in China by Leo Paper Group

ISBN 978 1 4062 1011 8 (hardback)
ISBN 978 1 40621 021 7 (paperback)

12 11 10 09 08
10 9 8 7 6 5 4 3 2 1

British Library Cataloguing in Publication Data
Shuter, Jane
  The story of Roman invaders
  1. Romans - Great Britain - Juvenile literature
2. Great Britain - History - Roman period, 55 B.C.-449 A.D. -
  Juvenile literature
  I. Title

936.1'04

Acknowledgments
The publishers would like to thank the following for permission to reproduce photographs: ©AKG-Images/Erich Lessing p.6; ©Alamy p.19 (Robert Estall photo agency); ©The Art Archive p.17 (Archaeological Museum Ostia, Gianni Dagli Orti); © Bridgeman Art library p.16 (National Museums of Scotland), 15 (National Trust Photographic Library), 18 (Private Collection); ©Corbis p.8 (The Gallery Collection)

Cover photograph reproduced with permission of ©AKG-Images (Nimatallah)

Every effort has been made to contact copyright holders of any material reproduced in this book. Any omissions will be rectified in subsequent printings if notice is given to the publisher.

Contents

Some words are printed in bold, **like this**. You can find out what they mean in the glossary.

Who were the Romans?

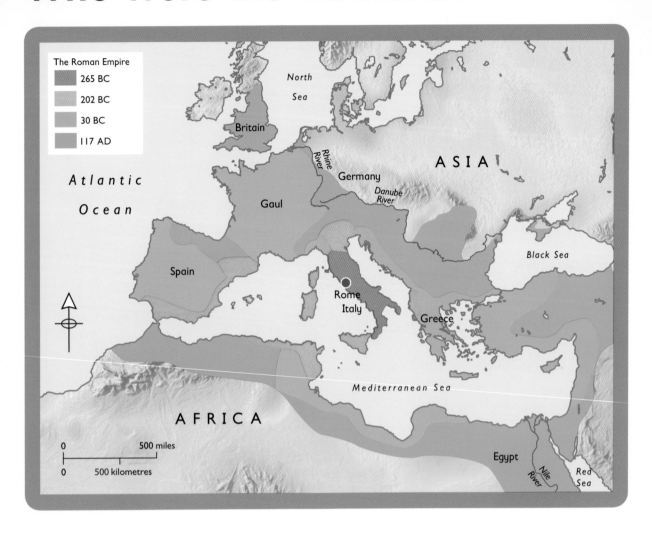

The Romans lived in Italy a long time ago. They began to take over land in 509 BC.

The map above shows how their **empire** grew. It was at its biggest in AD 117. After this, they began to lose land. Other countries took land from them.

The Romans needed an **army** to **invade** and **conquer** other countries. Roman soldiers fought in **legions**. They were well equipped and well trained.

The picture shows what a legionary, an ordinary Roman soldier, wore to fight.

spear

helmet

armour

sword

shield

Invading Britain

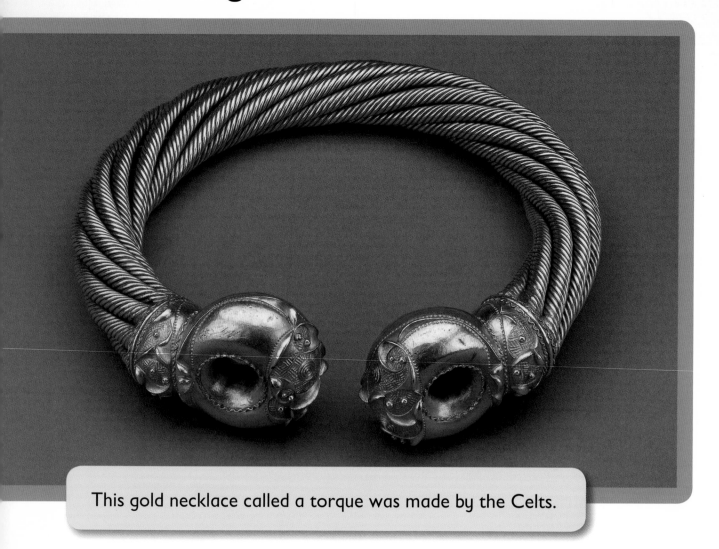

This gold necklace called a torque was made by the Celts.

In AD 43, the people in Britain were called **Celts**. They lived in small villages and farmed the land near by. Their round houses had thick roofs and walls to keep the cold out.

The Celts were clever and skilful. They made many beautiful things.

A modern artist's view of a Celtic village.

The Celts lived in small groups called **tribes**. Tribes often fought each other. The Romans **invaded** Britain in AD 43. They invaded Britain because they wanted to stop the Celts from helping other tribes in the Roman **Empire rebel**. It was hard for the tribes to work together to fight the Romans.

Fighting the Celts

The **Celts** did not have trained armies like the Romans. All the men of the **tribe** fought when there was danger. Some women fought, too.

The Celts fought with swords and spears. They had shields, but they did not have armour.

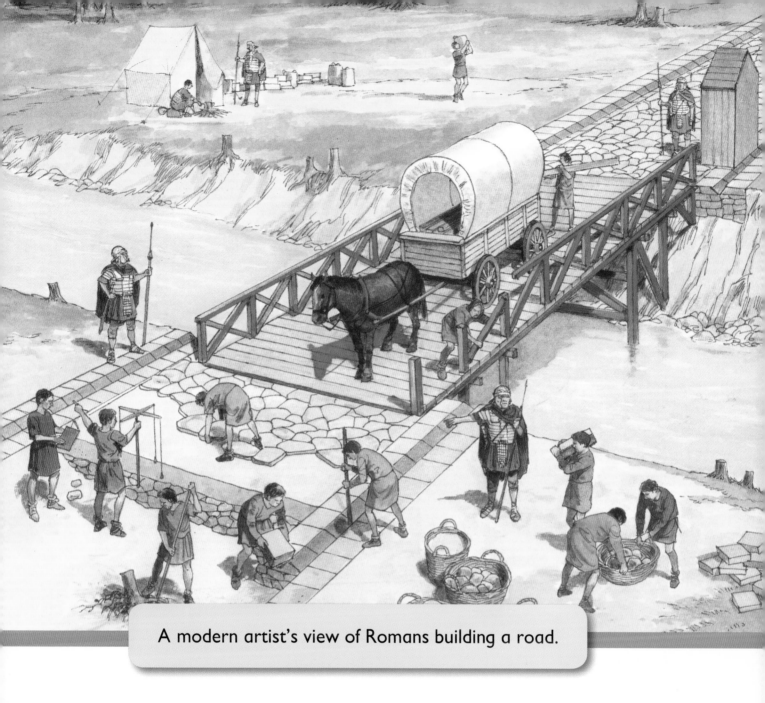

A modern artist's view of Romans building a road.

First the Roman **army invaded** the south of Britain. Then they moved north, adding more and more of the country to their **empire**. As the Romans took over, they built forts to keep the army safe and roads so the army could move quickly.

Fighting back

Some **Celts** accepted the Romans as their rulers. Others wanted to fight the Romans.

In about AD 60, Queen Boudicca led several **tribes** to attack Roman towns. They burned Colchester, St Albans, and London. Many people were killed.

A modern artist's view of Boudicca and her warriors.

More Celts joined Boudicca's **army**. Then the Romans made a clever plan and beat the Celts in a big battle. Boudicca killed herself. The tribes broke up. The **rebels** had failed. Some of the Celts from the tribes then accepted the Romans and their way of life.

Roman towns

Even small towns like this one had theatres.

When the Romans **settled** in Britain many things changed. The Romans built roads, bridges, and towns. Roman towns had streets that were paved with stone. The **forum** was an open space in the middle of the town. It had shops and the town was run from the **basilica** there. **Temples** for the gods were nearby.

Rich and important people used more expensive bath houses.

Towns had **public baths**, where everyone could wash and use the toilet. Bath houses had rooms that were warm, hot, and cold. They had warm and cold pools to swim in, too.

The Romans did not use soap. They put oil all over their bodies, then scraped it, and the dirt, off.

Roman villas

A modern artist's view of a rich Roman's villa.

Rich people had big farms and homes in the countryside, called **villas**. Villas had rooms built round a garden. Some also had their own **bath houses**. There were lots of **slaves** to look after the house and farm the land.

Villas and bath houses were warmed by a **hypocaust** system. Wood was burned to make hot air that moved around a space under the **mosaic** floors. This was the first ever kind of central heating!

Roman religion

The Romans believed in many gods and goddesses. They were happy to add more when they **conquered** a country.

When they **settled** in Britain they started to believe in the locals gods, too. They did not make the **Celts** change their religion.

A statue of Brigantia, a Celtic goddess, dressed in Roman robes.

The Romans decorated their basilicas with pictures of Christ.

In AD 391, the emperor said everyone in the Roman **Empire** had to become **Christian**. They turned many of their **basilicas** into churches. Christians believe in one God. No other gods were allowed. Christianity then became one of many British religions.

The Romans leave

This artist used their imagination, not evidence from the time, to paint the Romans leaving.

The Roman **Empire** got too big to control. **Tribes** inside the empire began to **rebel**. Tribes from outside began to attack. Roman soldiers were needed in Rome.

The Roman **army** left Britain in AD 407. Slowly, most other Romans followed.

A surviving Roman road near Manchester.

People in Britain started to live in tribes again. They returned to living in villages and farming the land around. The Romans who stayed in Britain also began living like this. Roman towns and **villas** were left to fall apart. People still used the Roman roads to get around and some still **survive** today.

Teachers' guide

These books have followed the QCA guidelines closely, but space has not allowed us to cover all the information and vocabulary the QCA suggest. Any suggested material not covered in the book is added to the discussion points below. The books can simply be read as information books, or they could be used as a focus for studying the unit. Below are discussion points grouped in pairs of pages, with suggested follow-up activities.

PAGES 4–5

Talk about:
- Discuss why people move to live somewhere else. Discuss the words 'immigration', 'emigration' and 'settle'. Explain the difference between invading and settling. Explain what an empire was and discuss why the army was so important to empire building.

Possible activity:
- Brainstorm reasons why the Romans might have wanted to build an empire. How would it be good for the Romans? What problems might it create?
- Mark the Roman period in Britain on the class timeline.

PAGES 6–7

Talk about:
- Discuss how the Celts might have felt about the invaders. Remind the children that Celtic tribes often fought each other – how would this help the Romans? Explain that the Romans saw most non-Roman groups as barbarians and not civilised because they did not live in the Roman way. Discuss how the Celtic way of life suited Britain: houses were low with thatch that sloped so the rain could run off and thick walls to keep the warmth in.

Possible activity:
- Use the artwork on page 7 to draw a Celtic house on a piece of paper, leaving room around the edges. Label the features that were suitable for the climate.
- This could be used to introduce citizenship work on judging other cultures. Maybe through a debate on whether the Romans were right to think that all other people were barbarians.

PAGES 8–9

Talk about:
- Discuss the picture on page 8: which one is the Roman legionary, which the Celt – cross reference skills to legionary artwork on page 5. What can we see in the background (Celtic house?) Tell them about hill forts, used by the most important leaders and used by nearby villages in emergencies. Stress that there were many, many more villages than hill forts.

Possible activity:
- Role play: tell the children you are a new recruit to the Roman army and they are experienced Roman soldiers. Ask them why soldiers have to waste their time building roads (depending on how quickly they respond ask more questions to guide their responses).

PAGES 10–11

Talk about:
- Discuss the fact we know very little about Boudicca: people even spell her name differently. Read the children the description of Boudicca by Dio Cassius. You can find one at http://czv.e2bn.net/e2bn/leas/c99/schools/czv/web/boudicca4.htm. He never saw Boudicca, but says he spoke to people who did.

Possible activity:
- Try to draw a picture of Boudicca based on the evidence in the source.

PAGES 12–13

Talk about:

• Discuss how settlement is different from invasion: trying to provide a comfortable way of life, not just hold on to the country. Remind them that they worked out that Celtic buildings were suitable for the climate. Discuss why the Romans brought their kinds of buildings and their way of life to Britain, rather than just changing to British ways (Roman ideas of 'civilized' life; showing they are in control).

Possible activity:

• Make lists of the similarities and differences between the Roman town on page 12 and the Celtic village on page 7.

• Make a copy of the layout of Colchester without the labels (from http://www.romans-in-britain.org.uk/arc_roman_towns.htm). Discuss where the forum, temples and basilica may have been.

PAGES 14–15

Talk about:

• Stress that villas could be very grand, as on page 14, or much smaller and simpler. They always had farmland attached. They were almost always built in the Roman style, around a courtyard, with a bathouse. Explain that the quality of mosaics varied according to how much people could pay. Simple black and white patterns were cheapest. The more colour you used, the more complicated the design was and the smaller the pieces of tile, the more expensive the mosaic was. http://www.romanbritain.freeserve.co.uk/villa.htm has a good discussion of Roman villas at an adult level and plans you could use for extension activities.

Possible activity:

• Design a poster for a builder advertising his villa-building skills, OR design two mosaic floors, a cheap one and a very expensive one.

PAGES 16–17

Talk about:

• Discuss the difference between having a religion that has many gods and goddesses and one that has only one God that everyone has to believe in. Why would it be a good thing for the Romans not to make the Celts change their religion? When the Roman Empire became Christian, the Romans did not try to make everyone in Britain become Christian – they were already losing control of the country.

Possible activity:

• Find out more about Roman gods, goddesses and religion at http://www.bbc.co.uk/schools/romans/religion.shtml

PAGES 18–19

Talk about:

• Discuss the effect of the Romans on us now. You might want to display photos of buildings in this country influenced by Roman building styles. Give the children a list of words that have come into English from Latin and discuss some Latin stems to make the exercise easier (examples of words from various sources at http://pearsonlongman.com/dictionaries/pdfs/Words-Pour1.pdf,. Look in dictionaries for words with stems such aqua- cent- and equ-).

Possible activity:

• Find four words that have come from Latin.

Local history work

You could do some work on the Romans in your area. Local libraries and museums will have resources to help. If you live somewhere where the Romans did not settle, the reasons for this could become the focus of your enquiry.

Find out more

Books

New Explore History: Romans, Anglo Saxons and Vikings in Britain, Haydn Middleton (Heinemann Library, 2005)

The Life and World of Julius Caesar, Brian Williams (Heinemann Library, 2003)

Picture the Past: Life in a Roman Villa, Jane Shuter (Heinemann Library, 2005)

Roman Invasion: My Story, Jim Eldridge (Scholastic, 2008)

Step-Up History: Roman Invaders and Settlers, David Thorold and Simon West (Evans Brothers, 2006)

You Are In: Roman Britain, Ivan Minnis (Raintree, 2004)

Websites

www.bbc.co.uk/schools/romans/
Activities, timeline and resources about the Roman invasion of Britain.

www.bbc.co.uk/wales/celts/factfile/
Stories and games about the Celts and Romans in Wales.

www.museumoflondon.org.uk/
Find out how London did not exist before the Romans invaded!

Glossary

army soldiers who fight for a country

basilica building where the officials of a town met to make decisions and run the town

bath house place with several rooms of different temperatures that the Romans used to wash in. Often a bath house had toilets, too.

Celt one of the people who lived in Britain before, during, and after the Romans invaded and settled

Christian someone who believes in the teaching of Jesus Christ and in one God

conquer beat someone in a fight

empire a country and all the lands it controls

forum open area in the middle of a town

hypocaust way of heating rooms by moving hot air around a space under the floor

invade go into another country, with an army, to take it over

legion the Roman army was organised in legions. A legion was made up of about 4,800 soldiers and 1,200 workers.

mosaic small tiles put together to make a pattern or a picture

public baths big bath house in a town that everyone can use

rebel to rebel is to fight against the people running the country. People who do this are called rebels.

settle go and live somewhere

slave person who is not free to do what they like. They are bought and sold like a house or a car.

survive something survives if it is not destroyed. Something that has survived from Roman times can be seen today.

temple special building where gods and goddesses are worshipped

tribe group of people who all live in the same way and see themselves as belonging together

villa Roman house in the countryside, often with a farm and lots of land

Index